JESHI
the Gorilla

by Chelsea Gillian Grey
Illustrated by Christopher Leeper

AFRICAN WILDLIFE FOUNDATION®
KIDS!

To Miss Madison Elizabeth and Miss Shawna Anne, two young ladies who may write books of their own one day — C.G.G.

To Jack — C.L.

Published by Soundprints division of Trudy Corporation, Norwalk, Connecticut

Book design: Marcin D. Pilchowski
Book layout: Bettina M. Wilhelm
Editor: Laura Gates Galvin

First Edition 2005
10 9 8 7 6 5 4 3 2 1
Printed in China

Acknowledgments:
   Our very special thanks to Elodie Sampéré at AWF for all her graceful assistance, Mbake Sivha, wildlife expert, and all the staff at the African Wildlife Foundation.

Library of Congress Cataloging-in-Publication Data is on file with the publisher and the Library of Congress.

JESHI
the Gorilla

by Chelsea Gillian Grey

Illustrated by Christopher Leeper

Soundprints

Where Children Discover...

In a dense forest high in the mountains, a young gorilla named Jeshi sleeps in a nest made of soft, spongy moss and lush, green leaves.

As the sun rises, Jeshi stirs and opens her eyes. With a gentle rustle of leaves, she slowly sits up.

Jeshi stretches and looks around the dense forest high in the mountains. Sun shines through the treetops and onto Jeshi and her family as they wake and greet the day.

Jeshi is eight years old and she has a very big family—33 gorillas in all!

Jeshi reaches for a tender stalk of bamboo. She tugs it free and begins eating it. During early spring, bamboo is abundant and the gorillas eat their fill—it is their favorite food!

A short distance from her nest, Jeshi peeks through branches and hanging mosses to a small clearing. Geya, an older female in her group, has just given birth to not one, but two tiny babies!

The newborn twins are weak and helpless. Jeshi watches as Geya picks up one of the babies and cradles him against her stomach with one arm. The other lonely baby begins to softly cry. Geya cannot carry both babies at one time. She needs one of her arms to help her walk.

12

Jeshi watches Geya as she walks a short distance. The lonely baby's cries grow louder and louder. Geya puts the baby she is carrying down and walks back to the crying twin.

As soon as Geya reaches the side of the crying baby, the second baby begins to cry, too. Geya looks around frantically. She does not know what she should do!

Jeshi sees that Geya has a problem and she wants to help her.

Very slowly, Jeshi moves through the plants toward Geya and her babies. Geya makes a low, threatening noise. Even though Jeshi is part of her family, Geya is protective of her babies. Jeshi walks toward Geya carefully. Soon Geya understands that Jeshi means no harm to her babies.

Jeshi bends down and gently lifts one of the twins into her strong arms. She holds the tiny baby against her stomach and comforts her, cooing softly.

With the baby in her arms, Jeshi stands and waits. Geya watches Jeshi and understands. She moves back toward her other baby and lifts him onto her own stomach. Together, the two gorillas cautiously move back through the forest to the rest of their group.

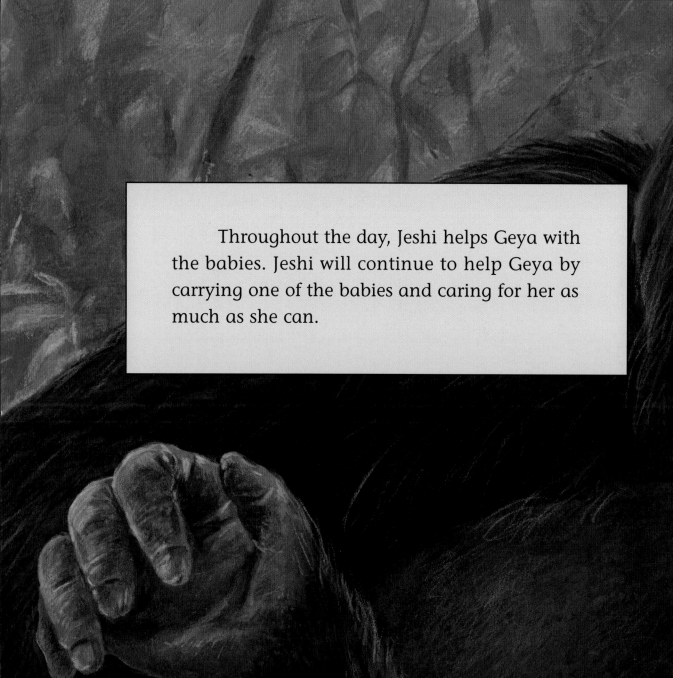

Throughout the day, Jeshi helps Geya with the babies. Jeshi will continue to help Geya by carrying one of the babies and caring for her as much as she can.

As the sun begins to fall behind the towering mountain, Jeshi and Geya return to their family group. Jeshi is only eight years old, but she now seems like a young mother!

Jeshi carefully pulls together a comfortable nest of branches, vines and mosses while she holds the baby in one arm. She snuggles next to the tiny baby gorilla, and soon they both drift off to sleep.

AFRICAN WILDLIFE FOUNDATION®
KIDS!

Would you like to learn more about Jeshi and other gorillas and animals in Africa?

Soundprints and the African Wildlife Foundation invite you to visit our website and sign up for monthly e-mail updates about Jeshi and other African gorillas.

Log on to:
www.awf.org/jeshi/

PRIVACY NOTE: Soundprints and the African Wildlife Foundation want to assure all participants who sign up for monthly updates on these fascinating animals that their e-mail address will be kept confidential and will be used for the sole purpose of sending these requested monthly updates from Soundprints and the African Wildlife Foundation. Under no circumstances will any information collected specifically for these e-mail updates be sold or distributed to any other organization for any other purpose.

Soundprints
Where Children Discover...

AFRICAN WILDLIFE FOUNDATION® KIDS!

ABOUT THE AFRICAN WILDLIFE FOUNDATION

For more than 40 years, the African Wildlife Foundation (AWF) has played a major role in ensuring the continued existence of some of Africa's most rare and treasured species. AWF has invested training and resources in African individuals and institutions that have played critical roles in conservation. The essential need to conserve Africa's remaining vital ecosystems inspired AWF to mark a new era in African conservation by establishing the African Heartlands Program. AWF Heartlands are large, cohesive land areas where governments, organizations, and individuals focus their joint conservation efforts. Ecologically, the Heartlands provide ample habitat for viable populations of wildlife to live, search for food and reproduce naturally. Economically, the Heartlands are increasingly valuable assets as wilderness becomes rare in our world. These wildlife attractions draw investors and offer enterprise opportunities that improve local economies and create wealth.

The African Wildlife Foundation, together with the people of Africa, works to ensure that the wildlife and wild lands of Africa will endure forever.

About Mbake Sivha, Wildlife Expert

Mbake Sivha is a conservationist committed to the never-ending struggle of saving the mountain gorilla. Mbake attended the University of Kisangani in the Democratic Republic of Congo, where she received her bachelor's of science degree. To further her education, she studied tropical biology and wildlife ecology at the University of Wuerzburg in Germany. Today she works with the International Gorilla Conservation Program (IGCP) to conserve gorilla habitat and improve the lives of the many people who live around the national parks in Uganda, Rwanda, and the Democratic Republic of Congo.

WHERE GORILLAS LIVE

UGANDA

CONGO

RWANDA

Virunga
Heartland

Gorilla Sites

AWF Heartland

Country Boundary

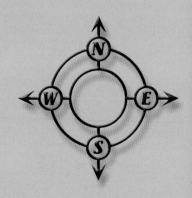

AFRICAN WILDLIFE FOUNDATION®
KIDS!

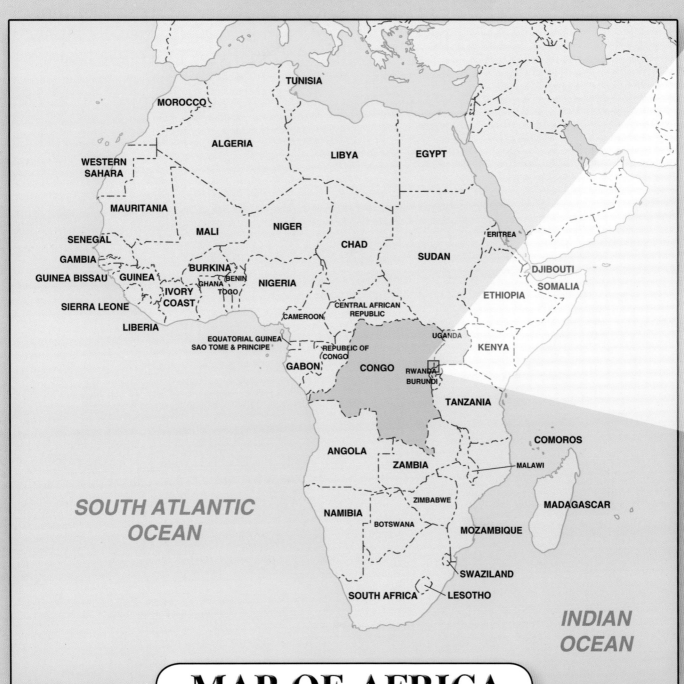

MAP OF AFRICA

About Mountain Gorillas

Mountain gorillas live in the dense, inaccessible rainforests of tropical Africa. They roam the areas near inactive volcanoes, eating certain plants, vines, fruits and tree bark. Mountain gorillas have very little interaction with humans.

Baby gorillas are born tiny, often weighing only 4 pounds. But they don't stay small for long. Full-grown female gorillas weigh 250 to 300 pounds, while the males grow twice as tall as the females and can weigh 450 to 500 pounds.

Contrary to popular belief, gorillas are not aggressive. In fact, they are shy and gentle, and live in close-knit family groups. They are highly social, and young gorillas play with each other very much like human children do.